What is Singapore?

LEVEL 3

by Ruth Wan-Lau

Illustrated by Eliz Ong

Published by Little Knights
An imprint of Armour Publishing
Block 1003 Bukit Merah Central #02-07 Singapore 159836
Email : sales@armourpublishing.com
enquiries@armourpublishing.com
Website : www.armourpublishing.com

19 18 17 16 15
7 6 5 4 3

Printed in Singapore

ISBN 978-981-4668-36-1

National Library Board, Singapore Cataloguing-in-Publication Data

Wan-Lau, Ruth, 1976- author.
Timmy & Tammy, what is Singapore? / by Ruth Wan-Lau ; illustrated by Eliz Ong. – Singapore : Little Knights, [2015]
pages cm. – (Let me read. Level 3)
ISBN : 978-981-4668-36-1

1. Singapore – Juvenile fiction. I. Ong, Eliz, illustrator. II. Title.
III. Series: Let me read. Level 3.

PZ7
428.6 -- dc23 OCN908527749

"What is Singapore?"

Timmy wants to know.

So, he asks his sister, Tammy.

Tammy does not know what

Singapore is.

So, she asks her friend, Raj.

What is Singapore?
?

Raj does not know what
Singapore is.
So, he asks his friend, Karim.
??
SINGAPORE
BOTANIC
GARDENS

Karim does not know what Singapore is.

So, he asks his friend, Quentin.

Quentin does not know
what Singapore is.

So, he turns to everyone and says,

"Let's ask an adult!"

“Mum, what is Singapore?”

Quentin asks.

“Singapore? Singapore is a

little red dot. A tiny island,”

Quentin’s mum says.

"It is small compared to the rest of the world, but it is a famous place."

"Dad, what is Singapore?" Karim asks.

"Singapore? Singapore is a large pot of soup. An exciting mix," Karim's dad says.

"It is full of people from around the world, but it is a harmonious place."

"Grandma, what is Singapore?" Raj asks.

"Singapore? Singapore is a butterfly. One that has just come out of its cocoon," Raj's grandma says.

"It has gone through tough times of change, but now it is a stable place."

“Grandpa, what is Singapore?” Timmy and Tammy ask.

“Singapore? Singapore is a porcupine. It is always ready to defend itself,” Timmy and Tammy’s grandpa says.

"It has many people
who will fight for it.
It is a peaceful place."

Timmy scratches his head
while Tammy rubs her chin.
"So, is Singapore a little red dot
or a large pot of soup?
"Is Singapore a butterfly or a
porcupine?" Timmy asks.

Everyone thinks for a moment. "Or, maybe, Singapore is a large soupy dot with wings and spikes?!" Timmy says.

Finally, Timmy says in a whisper,

"I know what Singapore is."

"What?" everyone asks.

"Singapore... "

what!!

" ... is like a dot. It is little because it is small enough to fit inside our hearts.

“Yet Singapore is like a large pot of soup. It is large because there is so much for us to learn about its past, present and future.”

"Singapore is like a butterfly. It can fly because we carry it in our hearts when we take a plane and go overseas.

"And, Singaporeans are like porcupines. We have spikes because we stand up for Singapore when we need to."

"Singapore is a little, large, flying, spiky place!"

Everyone laughs. And they all agree with Timmy.

"And not only that... "

Timmy and Tammy's grandpa says.

"… Singapore is OUR little,
large, flying, spiky HOME!
Singapore is OUR HOME."

Read all about Timmy & Tammy!

Level 1

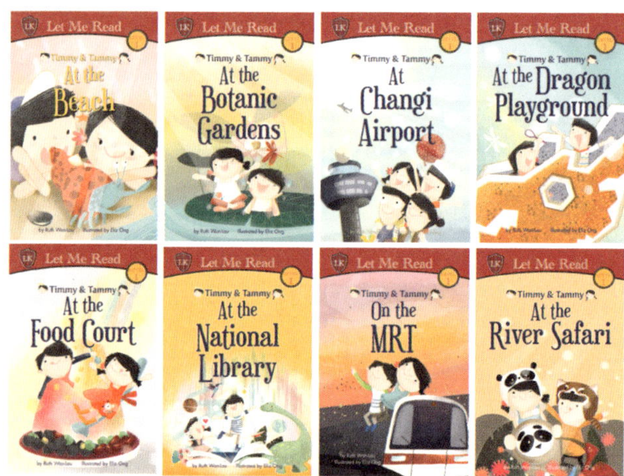

Level 2

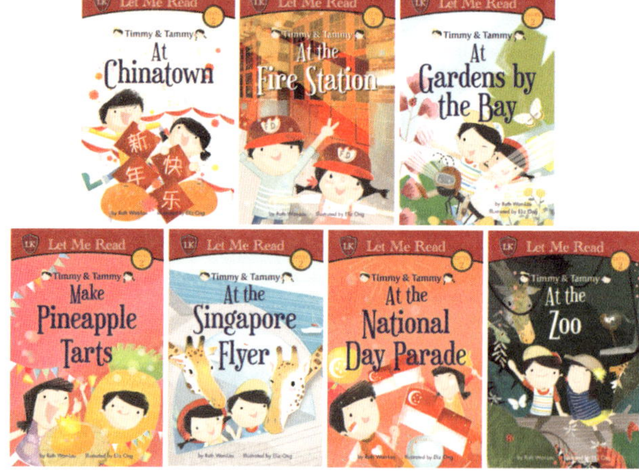

Level 3

Genius Level 4

The *Let Me Read* series is a guided approach to reading. The four levels of reading difficulty are:

Level	Description	Readers
LEVEL 1	* Beginning to read. * Sight words, words to sound out and simple sentences for new readers. Repeated words. * Familiar themes.	Emergent readers
LEVEL 2	* Growing readers. * Longer words and longer sentences. * Familiar and new themes.	Readers learning to decode
LEVEL 3	* Increasingly confident reading. * Simple chapters or stories broken into parts. * Familiar and new themes.	Increasingly confident readers
GENIUS LEVEL 4	* Confident readers. * Stories with several chapters. * Familiar and new themes.	Confident readers

The *Let Me Read* series uses large, clear type, while carefully matching text and pictures to ensure your child will have a smooth and enjoyable reading journey.

More in the *Let Me Read* series

Level 3

Genius Level 4

Dear Parent or Educator,

Emilie Buchwald said: "Children are made readers on the laps of their parents." The read-aloud experience is an adventure; it is an opportunity to bond with your child, while relishing the beauty of the printed word and colourful illustrations.

Here are a few tips for using the *Let Me Read* series:

* Read to your child with energy and enthusiasm.
* Read with your child. Allow your child to gain some level of confidence.
* Get your child to read to you or read to their younger (or even older) sibling. Celebrate little successes rather than being too mindful of errors in pronunciation or mistakes in phonetics.
* Think of the levels in this book as general recommendations. Know your child and be sensitive to his interests and preferences.

Most importantly, allow your child to be immersed in the book. Owning the words and seeing himself in the characters can make him think of the book as a friend, and see reading as the key to unlocking dream-like worlds.

Assistant Professor Myra Garces-Bacsal, PhD
Coordinator of MEd in High Ability Studies
National Institute of Education